RESCUES!

SANDRA MARKLE

Ⓜ MILLBROOK PRESS ◉ MINNEAPOLIS

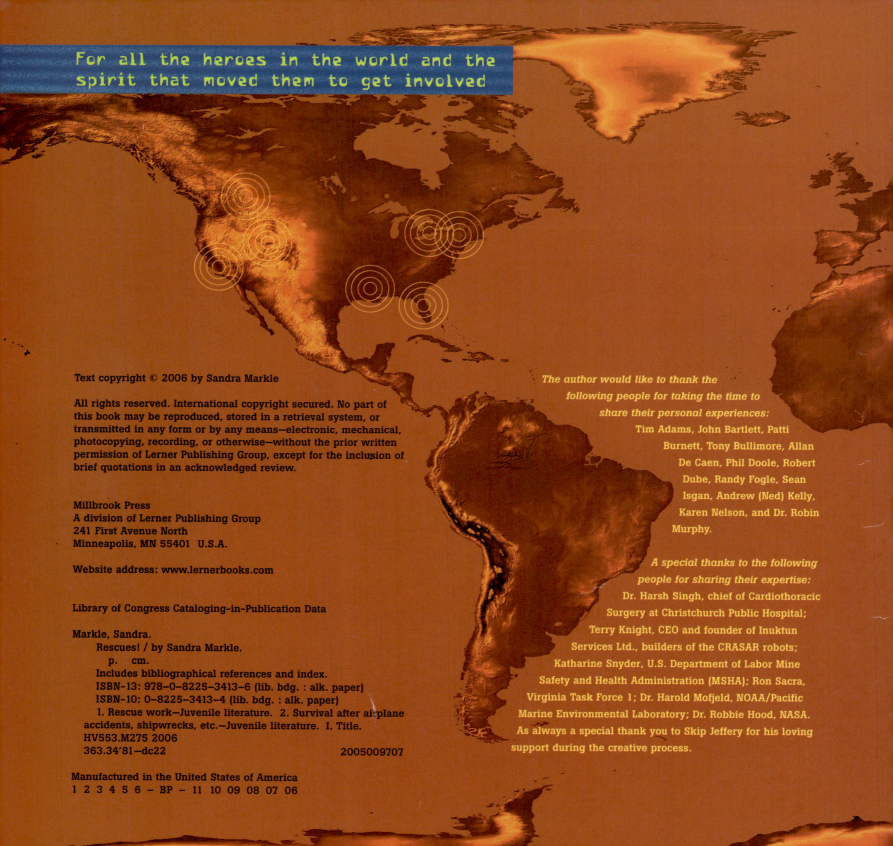

For all the heroes in the world and the
spirit that moved them to get involved

Millbrook Press
A division of Lerner Publishing Group
241 First Avenue North
Minneapolis, MN 55401 U.S.A.

Website address: www.lernerbooks.com

Library of Congress Cataloging-in-Publication Data

Markle, Sandra.
    Rescues! / by Sandra Markle.
        p.   cm.
    Includes bibliographical references and index.
    ISBN-13: 978-0-8225-3413-6 (lib. bdg. : alk. paper)
    ISBN-10: 0-8225-3413-4 (lib. bdg. : alk. paper)
    1. Rescue work—Juvenile literature. 2. Survival after airplane
accidents, shipwrecks, etc.—Juvenile literature. I. Title.
HV553.M275 2006
363.34′81—dc22
                                    2005009707

Manufactured in the United States of America
1 2 3 4 5 6 – BP – 11 10 09 08 07 06

*The author would like to thank the
following people for taking the time to
share their personal experiences:*
Tim Adams, John Bartlett, Patti
Burnett, Tony Bullimore, Allan
De Caen, Phil Doole, Robert
Dube, Randy Fogle, Sean
Isgan, Andrew (Ned) Kelly,
Karen Nelson, and Dr. Robin
Murphy.

*A special thanks to the following
people for sharing their expertise:*
Dr. Harsh Singh, chief of Cardiothoracic
Surgery at Christchurch Public Hospital;
Terry Knight, CEO and founder of Inuktun
Services Ltd., builders of the CRASAR robots;
Katharine Snyder, U.S. Department of Labor Mine
Safety and Health Administration (MSHA); Ron Sacra,
Virginia Task Force 1; Dr. Harold Mofjeld, NOAA/Pacific
Marine Environmental Laboratory; Dr. Robbie Hood, NASA.
As always a special thank you to Skip Jeffery for his loving
support during the creative process.

CONTENTS

NO ONE KNOWS WHEN DISASTER MAY STRIKE.

A storm, an earthquake, an avalanche, a wildfire, or some other natural event suddenly puts people in terrifying situations. Sometimes people accidentally get themselves into trouble too. Either way, the danger can be life threatening. In this book, you will find dramatic, real-life stories of people struggling to survive a disaster. The stories also tell of the efforts of trained professionals and everyday heroes who help save them—sometimes by risking their own lives. And they show how science and technology help to make survival possible.

A U.S. Park Service rescue team practices mountain rescue techniques to be ready for real emergencies.

COPPER MOUNTAIN, COLORADO
NOVEMBER 23, 1994

HASTY TO THE RESCUE

Patti Burnett jumped from the Life Flight helicopter with her golden retriever Hasty at her side. Together they ran to where a group of skiers was trying to find a woman who had been buried by an avalanche.

Laura Thompson* had been lucky. The avalanche was nearly at the end of its powerful slide down the mountain when it overtook her.

She had been knocked down and buried beneath it, but it hadn't dragged her down the mountainside. With only a small amount of air trapped in pockets in the snow, she would quickly run out of air to breathe. If the rescue team was going to save Laura, they needed to find her and dig her out quickly.

Finding Laura wasn't going to be easy. There was no way to quickly pinpoint her location. The skiers who had been nearby knew only the general area where Laura had been standing when the avalanche rolled over her. All they could do was stick their ski poles into the snow to try to locate her body. It was like using a pin to find a single pea buried in a huge bowl of mashed potatoes.

Skiers, walking in a row, stick their ski poles into the snow to search for an avalanche victim.

*The victim's name has been changed to protect her privacy.

TRANSCEIVERS

Statistics show that an avalanche victim is much more likely to survive if rescued within an hour. Transceivers, which became available in the 1960s, hugely increased the chances of an avalanche victim being discovered in time. A transceiver, once switched on, sends out a continuous radio signal. When someone is buried, other members of that person's group or rescue team members can switch their transceivers to receive. Then the buried transceiver becomes a beacon. A trained rescuer can home in on the strongest point of the transceiver's signal in just five to ten minutes. Then the rescuers can start digging.

avalanche!

An avalanche is a huge pile of snow and ice crashing down a mountain slope. An avalanche happens when heavy snowfalls build up layers of snow and ice on a mountainside. Then warm weather, wind, or even loud noises can start the piled-up snow and ice—sometimes tons of it—sliding. As the avalanche slides down the steep slopes, it picks up speed until it's traveling at hundreds of miles (kilometers) per hour. An avalanche will bury anything in its path. Sometimes an avalanche has enough force to crush houses as it roars down the mountain.

HASTY'S NOSE

Laura wasn't wearing a transceiver. Hasty, a trained avalanche search-and-rescue dog, was Laura's best chance of being found in time. Slipping off Hasty's leash, Patti told the dog, "Go find!" He immediately went to work, ranging back and forth across the snow, sniffing. He was searching for a human scent wafting up through the snow.

Dog's have a natural ability to detect a scent, categorize it, and store it for later recall. The way a dog detects a scent is to sniff, drawing the air and any chemical particles of odor that are in it into its nose. There a special fold just inside the nostrils opens to allow the air to flow across mucus-covered scent receptors. While different breeds of dogs have different numbers of scent receptors, dogs have an average of 200 million. (That's about forty times more than humans.) In fact, while human scent receptors cover an area about the size of a small postage stamp, a dog's scent receptors cover an area that would unfold to be the size of a handkerchief.

A dog's sense of smell works just like a human's. The scent receptors in the nose send signals to the brain. Once the brain analyzes those signals, which happens almost instantly, the dog becomes aware of the scent. Hasty wasn't born knowing how to zero in on a human scent, though. It was the result of Patti's long, patient training.

Patti and Hasty are ready to go into action to find a person buried under an avalanche.

TRAINING HASTY

When Hasty was only about two months old, the training began with runaway games. Patti encouraged Hasty to chase after her while she ran into the wind.

Next, Patti ran a short way and hid. Since Hasty had watched Patti hide, finding her was easy. But soon the game became harder. Hasty had to find someone hiding under a snow-covered tarp. Finally, he had to find someone buried inside a snow cave and help Patti dig the person out.

When Laura was hit by an avalanche, searching for avalanche victims was still like a game to Hasty—and it was one he was good at. Within just a few minutes, Hasty detected a human scent and started

Above: Hasty is training to find a victim buried under snow.
Below: The Life Flight nurse performs CPR on Laura during her rescue.

LIFE FLIGHT

Life Flight is an airborne ambulance. It may be a helicopter or a fixed-wing aircraft. The key is that the aircraft is able to quickly transport to hospitals patients who need critical care but are far away from care facilities. The Life Flight helicopter is equipped like an ambulance and staffed with specially trained nurses capable of providing intensive care at the scene of an accident and during transport. Life Flight helicopters often work in connection with search-and-rescue teams.

digging into the snow. Patti immediately called him. Digging for a long time in the icy snow could hurt Hasty's paws. The search party took over, using shovels. It wasn't long before they reached Laura and pulled her out.

AFTERWARD

Laura wasn't breathing, but she had a faint pulse. The Life Flight nurse who had arrived with Patti and Hasty immediately moved in to perform CPR (cardiopulmonary resuscitation, or reviving the heart and lungs). CPR involves temporarily breathing for someone by compressing the victim's chest and blowing air into the person's mouth, all at regular intervals. Almost immediately, Laura began breathing again, and her pulse strengthened. By finding her so quickly, Hasty had saved Laura's life.

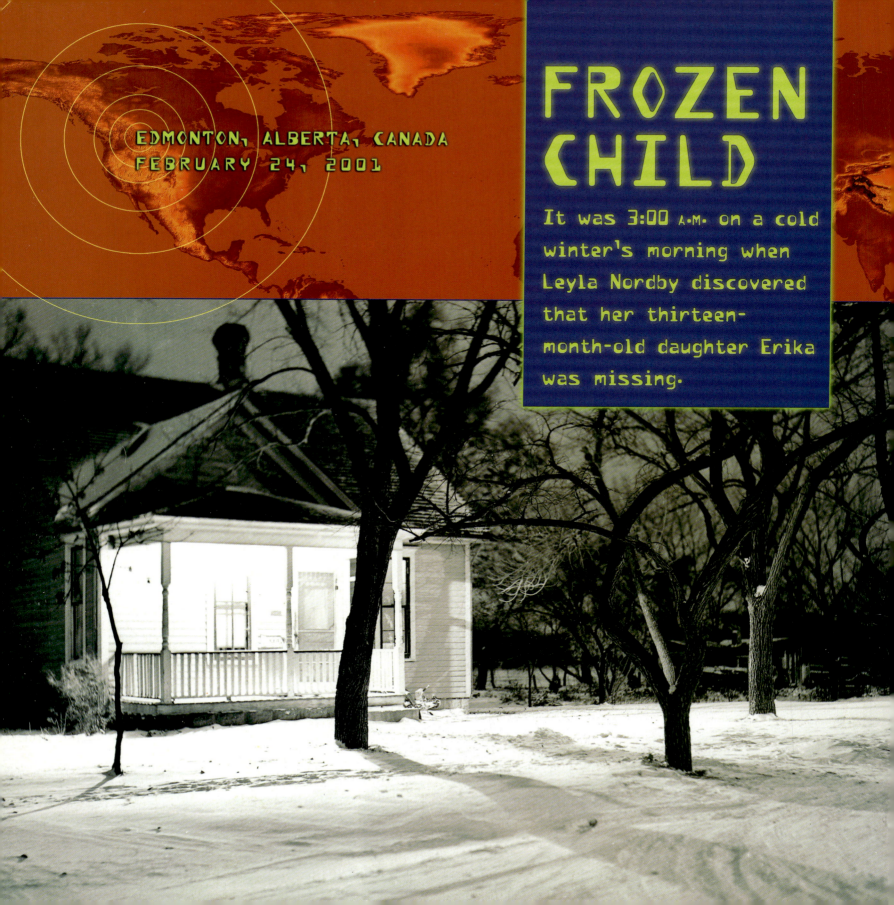

EDMONTON, ALBERTA, CANADA
FEBRUARY 24, 2001

FROZEN CHILD

It was 3:00 A.M. on a cold winter's morning when Leyla Nordby discovered that her thirteen-month-old daughter Erika was missing.

Leyla and her daughter were staying at a friend's house.
When Leyla went to sleep, Erika was in bed with her.

Leyla awoke and was stunned to discover her little girl wasn't there. While searching for the child inside the house, the worried mother found the back door open. Looking outside, she saw Erika lying in the snow, dressed in only a diaper and a T-shirt. Erika was stiff, pale, and unconscious. Leyla rushed her little girl into the warm house and called for an ambulance.

When the paramedics arrived, Erika wasn't breathing and didn't have a pulse. Her feet were encased in ice, and she had ice on her face and hair. One of the paramedics had worked on a similar case some years earlier. She knew that even though the toddler appeared to be dead, Erika might only be suffering from extreme hypothermia, or super heat loss.

Hoping that rewarming could save Erika, the paramedic started pressing on the toddler's chest. The paramedic's steady pressure,

HYPOTHERMIA

Hypothermia is what happens when the body's internal temperature drops below the normal 98.6°F (37°C). The body's first response is shivering, which is when the muscles contract in waves to try to generate body heat. This reaction becomes more violent as the body's internal temperature drops. The body shuts down blood flow to the surface skin, arms, and legs. The skin becomes pale, and the pulse and breathing rates slow. By the time the internal body temperature drops below 90°F (32°C), shivering stops. The heartbeat becomes irregular, breathing is shallow, and the person becomes unconscious. If the internal temperature drops below 86°F (30°C), the heart may stop. This may cause death. If the body loses heat quickly, though, its cells may retain enough energy to start functioning again when the body's normal temperature is restored.

followed by release, imitated the toddler's natural heartbeats. The paramedic hoped she could force the toddler's blood to circulate. The circulating blood would keep the little girl's body cells—and thus her heart, brain, lungs, and other vital organs—alive. While the paramedic continued to work on Erika, the rescue team rushed the little girl to Stollery Children's Hospital.

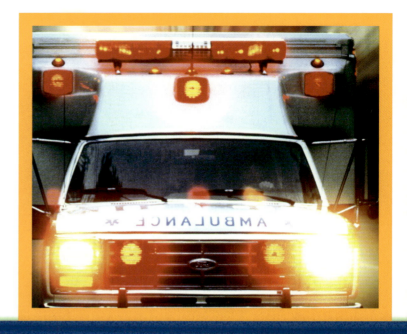

An ambulance rushes Erika to Stollery Children's Hospital in Edmonton.

LITTLE ICE GIRL

Dr. Allan De Caen, pediatric intensive care specialist, and his team were surprised by Erika's extreme condition. Her body temperature was very low— more than 30°F (16.7°C) below normal. However, a test to determine if the heart was still functioning showed that there was a small bit of muscle activity. It wasn't enough for the heart to pump blood on its own, but it gave the team hope.

Dr. De Caen said, "I knew if we were going to save her, we had to warm Erika up fast! With her body so cold, her heart had to be like frozen Jello. And every minute that went by without it pumping increased the chance her organs would start dying." Dr. De Caen decided he would have to put Erika on a heart-lung machine. This machine would temporarily take over the jobs performed by both her heart and her lungs.

THE HEART-LUNG MACHINE

The heart-lung machine takes over the jobs performed for the body by the heart and the lungs. The heart's job is to pump the body's blood to the lungs and then to pump the blood throughout the entire body. The lungs' job is to pass oxygen, a gas the body's cells need to live and function, into the blood. The oxygen is exchanged for blood's waste—carbon dioxide. This happens when oxygen from the air breathed in is passed into the blood, and carbon dioxide gas in the blood is passed into the air being breathed out.

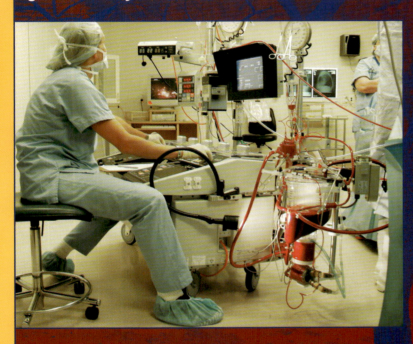

To take over the jobs of the heart and lungs, the body's blood is first pumped through a series of chambers in the machine. There, carbon dioxide waste is removed. Next, the blood passes into a special part of the machine where oxygen bubbles through the blood. The oxygen is picked up by the red blood cells just the way it would be in the lungs. This oxygen-rich blood also flows through a filter to remove any air bubbles that could damage the body. Then, acting just the way the heart would, the machine pumps the blood back into the aorta, the body's main blood vessel. From there, the blood travels throughout the rest of the body. In addition to being filtered and enriched with oxygen, the blood can also be cooled or warmed as it travels through the machine.

In the process, the machine would also warm her blood as it circulated through the machine. The warmed blood would help warm her whole body.

The heart-lung machine seemed to be the answer to quickly rewarming Erika's frozen body, but this treatment was also risky. Erika would have to be given Heprin, a powerful drug that thins the blood and keeps it flowing freely. A side effect of the drug is that the thinned blood could cause bleeding inside Erika's brain. But Dr. De Caen decided that was a risk that had to be taken. Other warming methods, like hot water baths and warm blankets, would take four to five hours longer to restore the little girl's body temperature to normal. That would be too long for the cells of her heart and brain to continue to survive.

STOP!

It took an hour for Dr. De Caen's team to prepare Erika for the surgery to connect her to the heart-lung machine. During that time, her body temperature only rose a few degrees. But just as Erika was about to be injected with Heprin, her heart started to beat. Her heartbeat was very slow, but it was steady. The surgical team decided the heart-lung machine wasn't needed. Instead, the doctor put Erika in the Bair Hugger, a giant plastic bag connected to a blower that kept

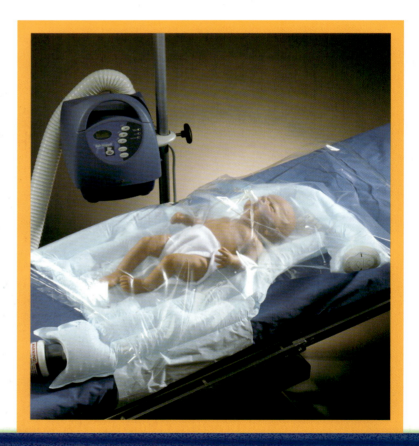

Erika was placed in a Bair Hugger like this one to warm up.

warm air circulating around her.

Slowly over the next four hours, Erika's body temperature returned to normal. To everyone's delight, the little girl was soon wiggling her fingers and toes. The medical team—Dr. Nadeem Milan, Dr. Allan De Caen, and Dr. Gary Lobay—checked her frequently during the next twenty-four hours. Finally, Erika moved on her own and squeezed her mother's hand. Leyla wept and hugged her daughter. The nurses and doctors wept too.

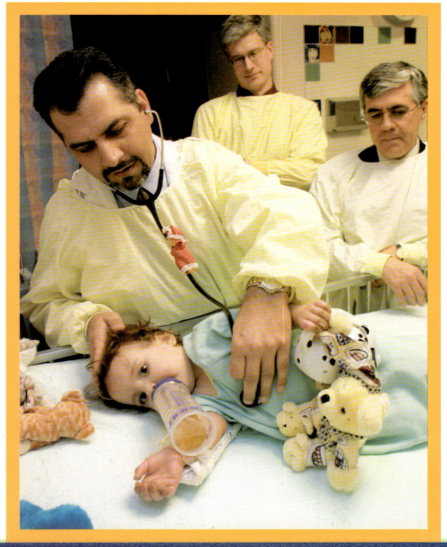

The medical team at Stollery—Dr. Milan (left), Dr. De Caen (center), and Dr. Lobay (right)—often checked Erika's condition.

AFTERWARD

Erika remained in the hospital for almost a month and required some minor plastic surgery. Frostbite (skin damaged when its cells became too cold to receive oxygen-rich blood) had affected her hands and feet, but she didn't lose a single finger or toe. Tests also showed she had not suffered any brain damage.

Erika is now perfectly healthy. No one would ever guess by looking at her that one cold night she nearly froze to death.

By the spring, Erika was ready to play outdoors with her mother.

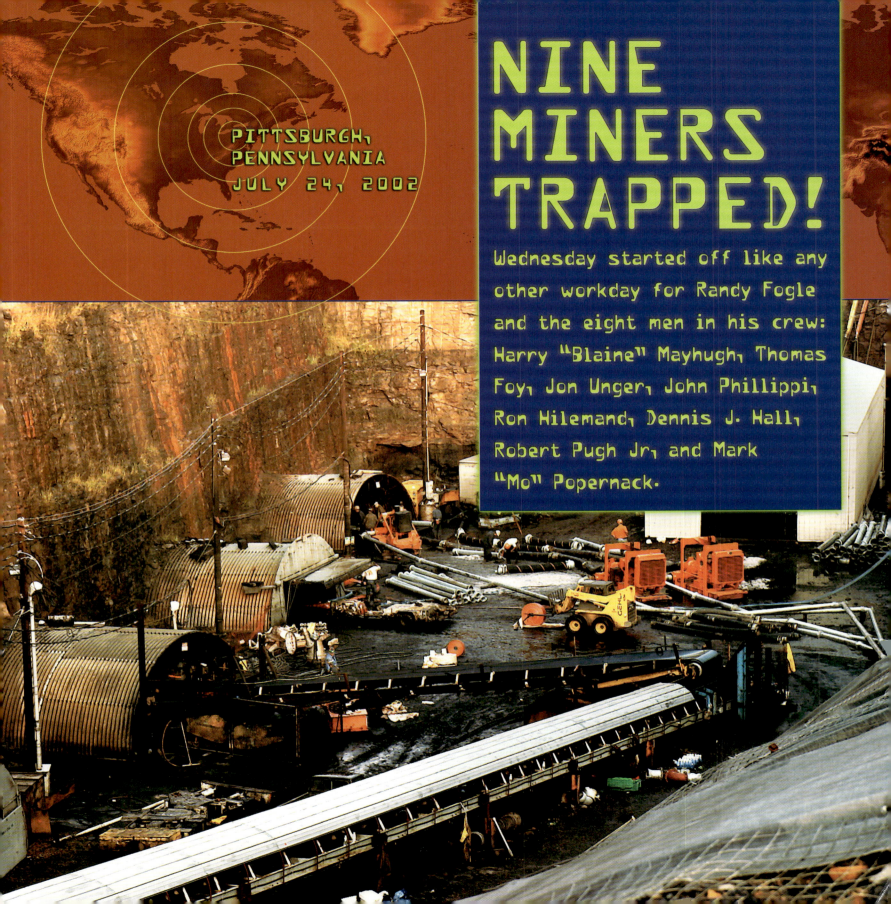

PITTSBURGH,
PENNSYLVANIA
JULY 24, 2002

NINE MINERS TRAPPED!

Wednesday started off like any other workday for Randy Fogle and the eight men in his crew: Harry "Blaine" Mayhugh, Thomas Foy, Jon Unger, John Phillippi, Ron Hilemand, Dennis J. Hall, Robert Pugh Jr, and Mark "Mo" Popernack.

At 3:00 P.M., at the beginning of the evening shift, the workers entered the Quecreek Mine near Pittsburgh, Pennsylvania. They left daylight and the summer's heat behind and descended 240 feet (73 meters) into the mine.

The shaft that Fogle's crew was working in was only 4 feet (1.2 meters) high, so they had to walk and work bent over. It was also only about 12 feet (3.6 meters) wide—not much wider than the mechanical miner, the machine that was carving its way through the coal seam. The front of the miner machine was a spinning cylinder packed with one hundred sharp bits, points that ground noisily as they dug out the coal. At the other end was a giant fan, roaring like a jet engine as it sucked in the dust. Down the center ran a conveyor belt loaded with coal. With its chain clanging, the belt hauled the coal back to railcars that would carry it out to the mine's entrance.

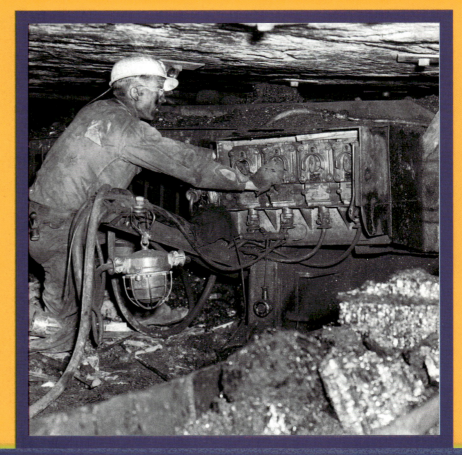

That night, like all the other nights, the men set to work. Soon they barely noticed the familiar noises of the miner. Suddenly, though, there was another sound that was terribly out of place.

The human miner adjusts the controls on the miner machine, which automatically digs out coal.

Randy Fogle said, "I was around the corner from the machine, but I knew what had happened. We'd hit water."

As water gushed through a hole in the shaft's wall, the miners started running away from it—back up the mine shaft. As he ran, Jon Unger got on his portable radio to warn the others behind them in the shaft. "Water coming! Water coming!" he yelled.

The men and the water both ran in the same direction—downhill. The men ran toward the elevator that could take them to the surface and safety. The water ran toward the lowest point in the mine, which was under the elevator shaft. The water was winning the race. When the water rose to waist depth, the men slowed to a crawl. They climbed up onto the conveyor belt and kept going. Even though they struggled to go as fast as they could, the icy water still beat them. Before the men reached the mine's lowest point, the water had already filled that section to the ceiling. It looked as though they were standing on the edge of a lake. And now the water was backing up. The lake was becoming bigger each second.

"This way!" Ron Hilemand shouted. The desperate men followed him down a side shaft that led to another exit, but the water was already flowing into this shaft too. The icy stream quickly became so deep that the miners were forced to swim back to the main shaft, keeping their heads close to the ceiling in order to breathe. Then all the men could do to escape the water was go back up the steeply sloping shaft they had just come down.

WHERE ARE THEY?

It was after 9:00 P.M. Wednesday night when civil engineer Sean Isgan and engineering technician Bob Long got the call that there had been an accident at the mine. They were told to go directly to the site of the accident, which turned out to be a pasture. There the Black Wolf Coal Company's officials were waiting for them. They showed Isgan and Long a map of the mine's underground network of tunnels.

"We think they're there," one of the company's executives said, pointing to the map. "That's somewhere under this pasture, but we need to know exactly where." It was going to take a big effort

Members of the rescue team meet with mine officials to determine the exact location of the miners trapped underground.

and a lot of equipment to drill deep enough to reach the trapped miners, so the rescue team needed to drill in the right spot as quickly as possible. Even if the miners didn't drown, they could die when they ran out of air. The part of the mine shaft that wasn't flooded was the only part that contained air for them to breathe, and the rising water cut the shaft off from any fresh supply of air.

Sean Isgan and Bob Long had brought along a GPS (Global Positioning System) unit. It would link them to a satellite network to pinpoint locations on the earth's surface. The mine company officials provided them with a map of the mine's shafts. This gave them the map coordinates for what should be the highest—and they hoped still dry—point in the shaft where the miners were trapped. The engineers entered that set of map coordinates into the computer and activated the GPS system.

HOW DOES THE GLOBAL POSITIONING SYSTEM (GPS) UNIT WORK?

Computers connected to the Global Positioning System are able to link up to satellites orbiting the earth. The computers are constantly within connection range of at least four of those satellites. So, for example, if you wanted to find out exactly where you are on the earth's surface, the GPS unit would first connect with one satellite to draw an imaginary circle connecting the earth and the satellite in space. That might determine that you are somewhere in the United States within a 550-mile (884-kilometer) radius from Washington, D.C. Next, the system would link up with a second satellite. Now there would be two circles that intersected at two points. This might determine that you are 550 miles (884 kilometers) from Washington, D.C., and 690 miles (1,110 kilometers) from Atlanta, Georgia. When the GPS linked with a third satellite, three circles would intersect at only one point—the exact location of the GPS unit on the earth's surface.

GPS location at the intersection of the three circles

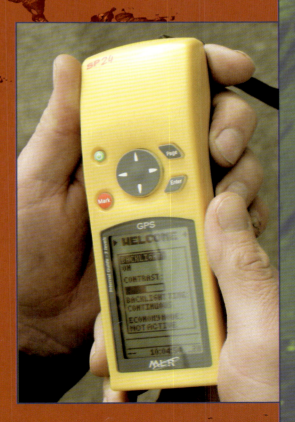

Then using a small handheld device called a "rover," which was linked to the GPS system, the engineers walked around the moonlit pasture. Their equipment signaled when they'd reached the point that matched the map coordinates.

The plan was to first drill a 6-inch (15-centimeter) hole. This small hole wouldn't be large enough to bring up the miners, but it could be drilled relatively fast. The rescue crew would know sooner that they'd drilled in the right spot, and they could pump air down to the trapped miners. A 24-inch (60-centimeter) hole would be needed to lower the rescue cage, a special bucket that could be used to lift the men one at a time to the surface.

Workers hurry to set up the drilling equipment that will let them reach the trapped miners.

The rescue team started drilling at the surface. Meanwhile, deep underground, the miners were hard at work, building a barricade to hold back the water. They were using 4-inch (10-centimeter) thick, solid concrete blocks that snapped together. Usually these blocks were used to build half walls to direct the air flowing through the main shaft into side shafts.

The men worked as fast as they could to collect the blocks and stack them up. But the water was rapidly backing up the shaft. Before the men were able to finish their barricade, the water surged around it and one section toppled over.

Discouraged, the miners retreated again. This time, they ended up back where they'd started—the highest part of the shaft.

NINE TAPS

In the pasture, the rescue crew worked hard to keep the drilling equipment going. Other crews were working hard too, pumping water out of the mine, to attempt to drain the mine shaft. But even with the pumps removing 20,000 gallons (91,000 liters) per minute, the water level was going down very slowly.

It took until Thursday, after seven hours of drilling and pumping, before the 6-inch (15-centimeters) pipe reached the mine tunnel. One member of the rescue team hit the pipe with a sledgehammer. The loud sound traveled down the pipe to the trapped miners. The rescuers became quiet, listening for a response each time the pipe was struck.

Randy Fogle said, "When we heard the noise, we scrambled toward it, and we found where the pipe had come through. I started tapping on the pipe. Then Mo tapped. He tapped nine times."

When the rescue team at the surface heard the nine metallic pings, they let out whoops of joy. They knew what this message meant. All nine miners were alive. Suddenly, as if an order had been issued, everyone on the rescue team went back to work. It was time to start drilling the big hole so they could get the nine men out of the mine.

SETBACK!

The miners stayed close to the pipe that linked them to the surface for as long as they could. But the water was still rising. After only a couple of hours, the men were forced to retreat again. The water had flooded the shaft up to where the pipe had punched through. The men moved back up to the highest point in the shaft—an area as small as an average-sized living room.

The end of the pipe connecting them to the surface was soon underwater, but it still played a vital part in the miners' survival. The rescue team continued to pump air down the pipe. Like air blown through a straw into a soft drink, the air bubbled into the water and through it into the air-filled pocket that was the men's refuge. This air created pressure in the shaft strong enough to stop the water from climbing any higher into it—for the moment at least.

Workers check the drill bit that is going to be used to drill a large rescue hole to the trapped miners. Then they attach the equipment to the drill that will be used for the escape tunnel.

The miners heard the distant rumble of the big drill bit grinding toward them through the earth. Randy said, "It sounded sweeter than music, but then it stopped." When the quiet minutes stretched into hours, the men wondered what had happened. They wondered whether the drill would ever start again.

At the surface, the rescuers worked frantically. When the hole was about 100 feet (30 meters) down, the drill bit became stuck in the rock and snapped off its shaft.

A replacement bit soon arrived by helicopter, but before drilling could resume, the men had to get the old bit out of the ground. When, after hours of effort, it looked as if that might not be possible, a second drilling rig was brought to the site. A second hole was started nearby.

Finally, on Friday, after more than eighteen hours of effort, the old drill bit was pulled up. Drilling resumed in the original hole, and the second crew kept drilling too—just in case.

When the first drill bit snapped off, a second one was rushed to the area.

BREAKTHROUGH!

The rescue crew broke into the mine shaft at 11:15 P.M. Saturday night. They'd timed it to happen just after the pumping crews finally succeeded in lowering the water level inside the mine. They hoped the water was low enough so the drill punching through to the shaft wouldn't burst the bubble of air that was holding back the water. If that happened, the water would rush into the space where the miners were waiting and drown them. Fortunately, the water level had been lowered enough.

The miners heard the sudden change in the drilling noise and guessed the drill had broken through. They switched on the two helmet lamps that were still working. Then they hurried to find the hole where they hoped there would be a rescue cage waiting to lift them to the surface. What they discovered was a cell phone dangling from a long wire.

Mo grabbed the phone and said, "Hey!" Then listening, he grinned. He said, "They want to know if they've reached the nine trapped miners."

The miners' laughter echoed off the rock walls. Randy asked, "They looking for somebody else down here?"

"It's us," Mo said into the phone.

One of the miners is brought up to the surface in the rescue cage.

At 1:00 A.M. Sunday morning—almost five days after he'd entered the mine—Randy Fogle climbed into the rescue cage and became the first miner to return to the surface. He was greeted by a wildly happy, cheering rescue team. Almost two hours later, when Mo Popernack became the last miner to escape the flooded mine shaft, the crowd was still cheering and wiping away tears.

Above: Mo Popernack was the ninth miner to be rescued.
Below: Randy Fogle is the only one of the miners who returned to working in the mines.

AFTERWARD

The Quecreek Mine is still operating. The miners had been stranded by the water because they accidentally punched into an abandoned, flooded mine shaft. To avoid a repeat of the disaster the nine miners endured, the Black Wolf Coal Company is working to track down all of the abandoned mine shafts. If they know where these shafts are, they can keep from mining too close to them.

As for the miners, eight of the men have changed jobs. Only Randy Fogle has returned to the mine. "It's what I do," he said. "What happened was just an accident."

1,400 MILES
(2,253 KILOMETERS)
SOUTHWEST
OF PERTH,
AUSTRALIA
JANUARY 9, 1997

SAILOR AT SEA IN SINKING BOAT

Tony Bullimore was sailing alone aboard the 60-foot (18-meter) *Exide Challenger*. He was competing in the Vendée Globe Race, which is a solo around-the-world sailing race. But sailing solo was nothing new for him.

At fifty-six, he had many years of experience sailing on all of the world's oceans. This race had been going smoothly, with good weather. Even his first two days in the Southern Ocean near the frozen continent of Antarctica had gone well. Then the weather changed for the worse, and so did the whole situation.

The storm built slowly, giving Tony time to take down the sails, lash down anything that was loose, and put on the safety harness that anchored him to the boat. At first, Tony thought the storm wasn't going to be more than an annoyance, but it kept on building.

For more than ten hours, Tony steered the bucking *Exide Challenger* through the rough sea. As the day faded into night, the storm finally seemed to ease. Cold and tired, Tony decided it was safe for him to get a cup of hot tea. So he flipped on the automatic pilot, a special instrument that can be set to control the boat's rudder, the device that steers the boat. This would keep the boat sailing on its programmed course while he was below the deck in the boat's cabin.

Tony was on the steps heading belowdecks when a roaring sound made him look up. Even in the dark, he could see the monster wave, looming over the *Exide Challenger*. Realizing it was about to crash over the sailboat, Tony raced into the cabin and slammed the hatch shut so violently, he chopped off the tip of one finger on his left hand.

An instant later, the wave struck with explosive force, and the *Exide Challenger* rolled, tossing Tony off his feet. The sailboat rolled over so far that Tony felt the mast slam against the water. Then, just as the sailboat seemed about to right itself, he heard a loud cracking noise.

monster waves

For decades, monster waves (below) were thought to be a sailors' myth to explain why ships disappeared at sea. Then in December 2000, a project called MaxWave was launched.

It used two European Space Agency satellites to study wave heights. Within just three weeks, surprised researchers discovered that the satellites had already recorded ten monster waves—each one more than 81 feet (25 meters) high.

Researchers are still studying what may cause monster waves to form. So far, they have two main explanations. Some monster waves are caused by normal waves running into strong ocean currents. Others are caused by strong winds, such as hurricane winds, that blow for more than twelve hours. Being hit by a monster wave is dangerous because water has weight—the more water, the greater the force. Just one gallon (3.7 liters) of water weighs a little more than 8 pounds (about 4 kilograms). Imagine the weight of a monster wave nearly as tall as a ten-story building!

UPSIDE DOWN

The keel had snapped off. The keel is the fin-shaped projection on the bottom of a boat that keeps it upright. The boat did a complete somersault, tossing Tony off his feet again. This time, when the boat stopped rolling, it was upside down. One of the cabin's windows caved in from the pressure of water. As the seawater surged into the cabin, Tony thought the boat would sink completely. But when he was about waist deep in icy cold water, the boat stopped sinking. The air trapped inside the hull, the body of the boat, was keeping the boat from sinking any farther—for the moment.

Tony forced himself to think about what he should do to stay alive until help arrived. First, he put on his insulated survival suit. Unfortunately, he hadn't purchased the boots, gloves, or hood that went with the suit. So even as his body began to warm up a little, his feet (even with his shoes on), his hands, and his head were freezing cold. Desperate to get out of the cold water, he climbed up onto a little ledge—what had once been a shelf near the cabin's ceiling.

The next problem that Tony faced was a lack of food and water. Luckily, Tony found a little desalination pump in the cabin. This device allowed him to remove the salt from ocean water so that he would have freshwater to drink.

A monster wave capsized Tony Bullimore's sailboat.

Desalination Pump

A desalination pump is a device that pushes seawater through a very fine mesh filter to produce fresh—unsalty—water. The salt particles in seawater are too tiny to see without a microscope to magnify them, but they're still bigger than water molecules. So with a fine enough mesh, the salt particles are trapped as the water is pushed through the filter. Only freshwater comes through the other side of the filter. It's been estimated that it takes about one thousand pumping motions with the hand-pump desalinator to produce just 1 cup (0.3 liters) of drinkable water. But those one thousand motions can mean the difference between life and death.

The human body needs a little salt to function normally, but only about as much as a quarter teaspoon (1 milliliter) a day. Seawater is a lot saltier than that. When a person drinks seawater, the body's cells give off water in an effort to dilute this excess salt and wash it out with the urine. Because the cells are losing water, the body dehydrates, or becomes short of critically needed freshwater. Without enough water in the cells, a body can't function properly. The dehydrated person passes out, the kidneys stop functioning, and all of the body's organs are damaged. If the body's normal water level isn't quickly restored, the person is likely to die.

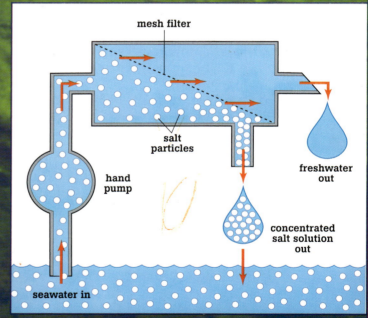

He also found a couple of candy bars. He ate one of the candy bars immediately and nibbled the other one slowly over the next day.

TRYING TO ESCAPE

By the end of the second day, Tony realized that the boat was sinking again. The mark he'd made on the cabin wall to show the water level was now underwater. He decided that his only hope to survive was to find a way to get off the *Exide Challenger*. He dove through the open cabin window and swam to the cockpit, the part of the boat with the steering wheel and control instruments. He knew there was an inflatable life raft there. He dove down to look for it and found it still attached to the ship. But the ropes holding it in place were wrapped around pieces of wreckage. He wasn't able to stay underwater long enough to untie them. He swam back to the cabin for a knife. Then he made a second dive, carrying the knife in his mouth, and tried to cut the life raft free.

He still wasn't able to do it, but he did something else that ultimately saved his life. He reached the distress beacon that was in the cockpit and flicked it on. The *Exide Challenger* was equipped with two beacons. The first was the one that had automatically switched on to "distress" mode when he capsized. The second was activated only when switched on by hand.

HE'S ALIVE!

Tony didn't know that, within hours of the boat's capsizing, the race's officials had realized the *Exide Challenger* was in trouble. At race headquarters, officials monitoring the progress of each of the boats had picked up Tony's beacon signal and that of Tony's closest competitor, Thierry Dubois. Both boats had been capsized by the same wave. The officials immediately launched a search-and-rescue operation.

A search plane spotted Dubois several hours later, sitting on his overturned boat. They dropped an

survival suit

Protective clothing is needed to stay alive in cold water. The human body cools down much faster in cold water than in air. Hypothermia, which happens when the body temperature drops more than just a few degrees, can make it difficult to swim, stay afloat, and even breathe. A survival suit (right) is an insulated suit made of special Neoprene and titanium fabrics designed to prevent heat loss. Because the suit is buoyant, it also helps a person stay afloat more easily. The suit is nicknamed the Gumby suit because someone dressed in this brightly colored suit has the general shape of the Gumby cartoon character. Unfortunately, Tony Bullimore's suit lacked the boots, gloves, and hood.

inflatable lifeboat he could climb into until help could reach him. The searchers in the plane also spotted the capsized *Exide Challenger*, but they reported no sign of Bullimore. Since no boats of other race competitors were close enough to conduct a rescue mission, race officials called on the closest ship, the Australian navy's HMAS *Adelaide*. The ship immediately headed toward the site of Tony's boat, but bad weather slowed the *Adelaide*'s progress.

Three days later, a rescue helicopter launched from the *Adelaide* rescued Thierry Dubois. The helicopter also circled the *Exide Challenger*, which was still afloat. But the rescue crew didn't see any sign of Bullimore, and they returned to the *Adelaide*. The *Adelaide* continued toward the sailboat hoping to be able to recover Bullimore's body. When the seas became rough again, the captain considered calling off the recovery mission. It was then that he received word that Bullimore's second distress beacon had been activated. That raised the hope that Tony Bullimore was still alive. The captain ordered the *Adelaide* to stay on course toward the *Exide Challenger*.

Not knowing help was on its way, Tony spent his fourth day inside the overturned sailboat, getting ready for the boat to finally sink. He figured he only had about a day left before the cabin would be underwater. He got out his life jacket and stuffed rope into a bag. He planned to swim out of the boat with this equipment, put on the life jacket, and tie himself to the overturned boat. His plan was to stay with the boat as long as it remained afloat.

Suddenly Tony heard a loud *whump-whump-whump* noise. Hope surged through him. Thinking the sound must be a rescue helicopter, Tony plunged through the broken window and swam to the surface. What he saw when he burst through the waves was a huge ship, the *Adelaide*, and a Zodiak, an inflatable speedboat. The Zodiak was coming toward him.

Waving his arms, Tony shouted, "Here I am!"

A diver from the search-and-rescue team swims toward Tony.

AFTERWARD

Tony Bullimore was a lucky survivor. Doctors feared they might have to amputate one of his feet, which had been frostbitten, but that didn't prove to be necessary. He has frostbite scars on his face and is missing the end of the finger he cut off when he slammed shut the hatch cover. But his love for sailing remains as strong as ever. He continues to race. Now, though, when he goes

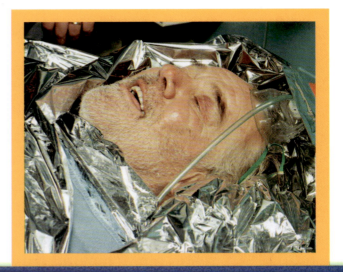

Tony (above) was wrapped in Mylar, a kind of plastic sheeting developed for astronauts, to keep him warm. Tony (below) recovered from his ordeal, and in spite of it all, he continues to race sailboats.

out to sea, he is ready for any emergency.

"In fact," Tony said, "I have a watertight box packed with survival gear, including a full survival suit and a radio. I have to keep believing something so desperate won't happen again, but now I'm better prepared in case it ever does."

BURIED ALIVE!

**TAICHUNG, TAIWAN
SEPTEMBER 21, 1999**

When the earthquake struck Taichung, Taiwan, it sounded like thunder. The ground rolled like waves on the ocean, and every building shook.

The powerful earthquake (7.6 on the Richter scale) shattered glass, heaved up streets, and burst water lines. It also collapsed buildings, turning them into mountains of broken concrete and steel.

Some of the buildings were high-rise apartment houses. Hsu Tse-kai was asleep in his bed in one of these high-rises. The bottom four floors of his twenty-story apartment building "pancaked," or fell down on top of one another. The remaining tower leaned over and came to rest on a neighboring building. Hsu Tse-kai ended up inside his rolled-up mattress, buried in a tangle of debris. But he was alive! Luckily, his head and part of his upper body were in an open space in the rubble. He began yelling for help.

Virginia Task Force 1's truck full of supplies is loaded onto the plane.

VIRGINIA TASK FORCE 1 GOES TO WORK

As soon as word of the Taiwan earthquake reached the United States, Virginia Task Force 1 was ordered to report for duty. As quickly as they could load people and equipment into a C-5 aircraft, this trained rescue team was on its way. They took along

earthquakes

The earth's crust is like the shell of an egg. The crust is cracked into pieces called plates. Under those plates, much of the earth's interior is believed to be rock melted to a fluid by the heat from the earth's hot central core. This molten rock moves and flows, and when

it does, it carries the plates along with it. Sometimes two of the plates lock together. Then pressure builds up until, like a stretched rubber band snapping back, one of the plates breaks loose and suddenly moves. Everyone living on the plate that moves feels it. That's an earthquake. Places near the edges of the plates have the most earthquakes. For example, Alaska has more than five thousand earthquakes a year—more than the combined total for the entire rest of the United States.

about 70,000 pounds (31,750 kilograms) of supplies. These included every kind of hand tool imaginable, medical equipment, lightweight protective gear (similar to what firefighters wear), tents, and food. The team was prepared to be completely self-sufficient at the disaster site for as long as ten days.

After a twenty-one-hour journey, the task force reached Taichung, and while they unloaded, advance teams went to survey the damage. Robert Dube was in charge of one of these teams. An interpreter told Robert about Hsu Tse-kai, and when his team got to the site, they discovered local people already there, attempting to dig him out.

Robert said, "We got down in their tunnel, and we could hear him talking. So we started using the local people's hand tools and called back for equipment."

AFTERSHOCKS STRIKE

Tunneling through rubble is like working a puzzle. But as a founding member of Task Force 1, Robert Dube was an experienced tunnel digger. With the help of Mike Istvan and Evan Lewis, he broke up the debris with hand tools and passed the chunks up to the surface. They were nearly 20 feet (6 meters) underground when the tunnel suddenly filled with dust. Robert said, "The next thing we know everything is shaking and

Members of Task Force 1 dig through the rubble.

falling. We start scrambling for the surface, and all the while the guy's screaming at us not to leave him."

By the time they reached the surface, the aftershock quake was over, and they went right back to work. When a second and then a third aftershock struck, they decided they couldn't make it out in time anyway, so they kept on digging.

The rescue team finally reached Hsu Tse-kai after two days of digging.

THE RESCUE

It took two days of nonstop effort to dig down into the wrecked building to reach Hsu Tse-kai. And it took eight more hours to free him from the rubble. Then the team strapped him to a Sked, a sturdy plastic stretcher, and hauled him to the surface. There, other rescuers took over. They rushed Hsu Tse-kai into an ambulance, and Robert Dube never saw him again.

Robert said, "When we got him out, he was happy, that's for sure. I know he survived. We heard that later." But by then, Robert Dube and his team were already busy searching for other survivors. They worked hard for eight more days, but Hsu Tse-kai was the only person they found alive.

LIFE DETECTOR

Most of the time, rescuers can't immediately hear victims trapped in earthquake rubble. That's when the Life Detector can help. It can pick up extremely small sound vibrations—like someone tapping on concrete or wood. Then it displays these

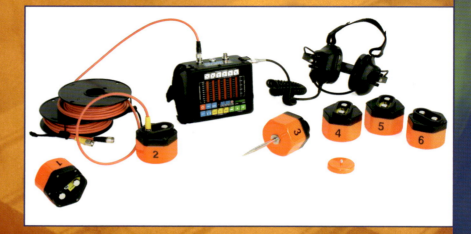

vibrations as a bar chart on a screen, the way a home stereo system displays sounds. To pinpoint the sounds, six sensors are arranged around a section of the rescue scene. Then the rescuer searches between the two loudest channels—the sensors picking up the strongest signals. Next, the ring of sensors is moved to within this focus area, and the process is repeated to narrow the search area. Digging through rubble is a huge job. The Life Detector makes it possible to home in on the exact place the victim is trapped.

Another system for rescuing earthquake victims takes advantage of the fact that many people carry cell phones. A Japanese company, Toshiba, developed an emergency system that can be activated in any area by a call to a special number. The system transmits an alert message to every cell phone in that area, causing them all to ring. Then rescuers can use the ringing phones as beacons to home in on.

AFTERWARD

Robert Dube followed his grandfather and his father into the fire service. He worked for the Fairfax County Fire Service in Fairfax, Virginia, for a number of years. And when Fairfax County started a search-and-rescue team, he joined that. This group eventually became the Virginia Task Force 1, handling international missions. Robert worked on  twelve different missions with Virginia Task Force 1, performing many different jobs, including rescue specialist, tool operator, and task force leader. But those missions required Robert to be away from his family for long periods. So finally, he decided it was time to stay home. Today, he is once again focusing on helping to keep one community safe. Robert is the deputy fire chief for Clearwater, Florida.

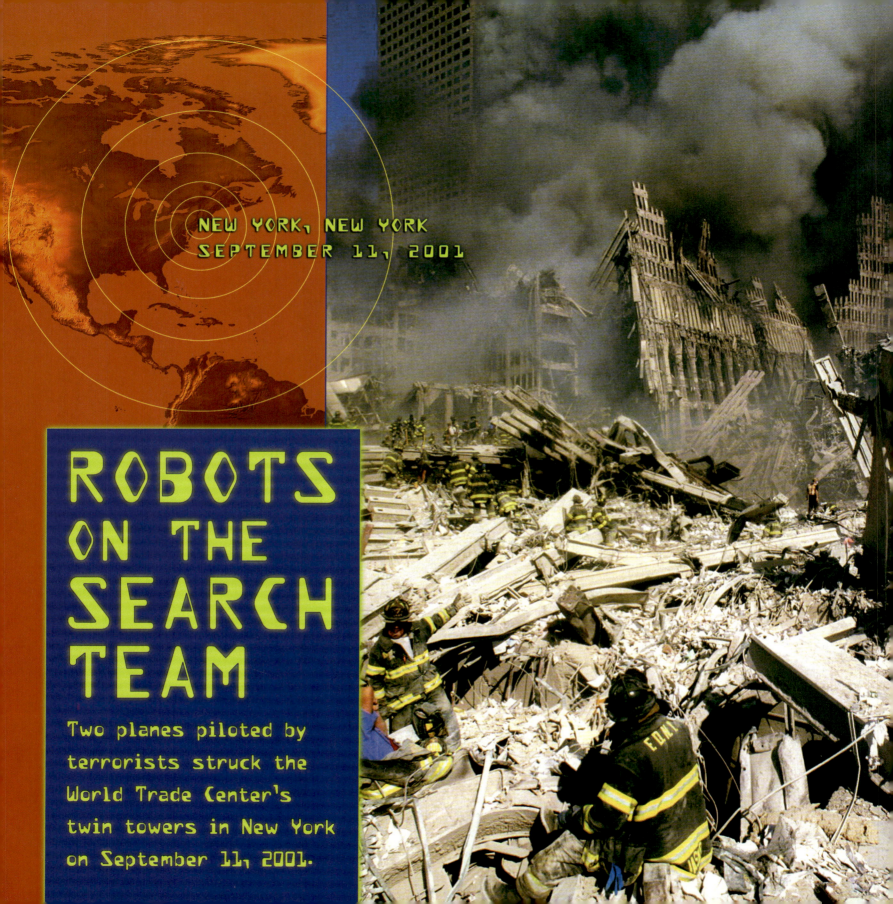

NEW YORK, NEW YORK
SEPTEMBER 11, 2001

ROBOTS ON THE SEARCH TEAM

Two planes piloted by terrorists struck the World Trade Center's twin towers in New York on September 11, 2001.

What had been the world's fifth- and sixth-tallest buildings turned into tons of twisted steel, broken concrete, shattered glass, and debris.

Worse, the rubble heaps were piled into pits that had once been the subway station and shops underground. Fires broke out after the initial impact. When human rescue teams started searching for people trapped in the rubble, the CRASAR (Center for Robot-Assisted Search and Rescue) robots soon arrived to help. These mechanical searchers had an advantage over human searchers and rescue dogs. Directed via remote controls, they can move into really small spaces and travel through places where the rubble might collapse.

The CRASAR robots are no more than 12 inches (30 centimeters) long and 6 inches (15 centimeters) wide. They can move along as flat as a mouse or stretch up as tall as a squirrel that's sitting up. This position enables the robot to "see" over objects with its cameras and also crawl up and over obstacles.

Once inside the rubble, the robots were able to explore more than 100 feet (30 meters) away from the control center.

CRASAR robots can flatten to squeeze through tight places or raise their lights and cameras to see over obstacles.

Their lights and cameras could be raised and turned to show their operator what was around them. Even elevated, though, the little robot's low viewpoint and

A CRASAR robot moves over the debris of a collapsed building on its tractorlike treads.

the amount of dust in rubble made it hard for the operator to recognize a human victim. The robots are also equipped with heat sensors and chemical sensors that detect carbon dioxide. Carbon dioxide is the waste gas people breathe out. When a robot detected both heat and carbon dioxide, the operator knew that the robot was close to a living, breathing person.

AFTERWARD

The CRASAR robots didn't find any living survivors at the World Trade Center. They did, however, help locate the bodies of five victims. The CRASAR team also gained insights that they are putting into practice so the mini-robots can be even more effective searchers in the future.

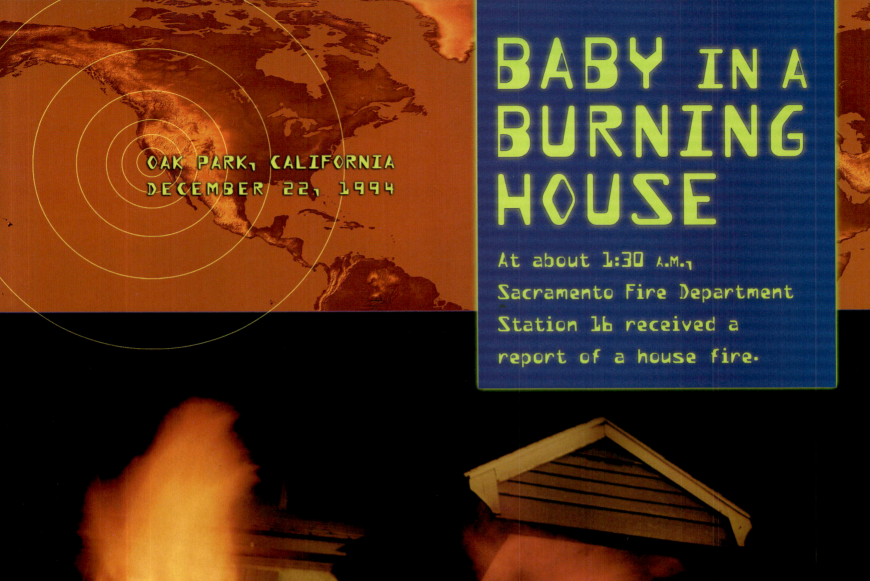

OAK PARK, CALIFORNIA
DECEMBER 22, 1994

BABY IN A BURNING HOUSE

At about 1:30 A.M.,
Sacramento Fire Department
Station 16 received a
report of a house fire.

The trucks were on their way back to the station from a medical call, but they immediately changed direction and headed out to handle this new emergency.

Even though the report hadn't included an exact street address, the driver was guided to the house by the plume of smoke rising from the burning building. When the fire crew arrived, the windows at the front of the house were glowing bright orange from the flames inside. Captain Tim Adams immediately got on the fire engine's radio to report the house's address and condition. Before he had finished, he was interrupted by people banging on the truck's door.

A fire engine races to a burning building.

"There's a baby inside!" a man shouted. "You've got to help!"

Captain Adams climbed out of the truck, and the man grabbed his arm. He explained that twenty-three-month-old Daishna was still inside the burning house. The man quickly guided Tim to the left side of the house. They went past a man spraying a garden hose at the left front window and down a driveway. The man pointed at

a broken window about head high and said, "The baby's in there!"

Tim grabbed the window ledge and pulled himself up to look inside. The hot air blasted his face as he looked into a bedroom. The room was so full of smoke that he couldn't see much. He could see flames rolling across the ceiling. He could also see burning clothes draped over an open closet door and flaming pillows on a glowing rectangle that he was sure was a bed. Tim thought, "Wow, there's no way there's anybody alive in there." Then he heard the baby scream.

Dressed for Fighting Fires

Firefighters dress to stay safe in extreme heat. The total weight of this gear is close to 100 pounds (just over 45 kilograms). That's before the firefighter picks up any equipment.

VISOR: This pulls down to provide face and eye protection.

HELMET: It may be leather or hard flame-resistant plastic. It has a bill in the back to keep water from running down the firefighter's neck.

SCBA (self-contained breathing apparatus): The tank, wrapped in fire-resistant fiberglass, contains compressed air to provide about thirty minutes of air to breathe.

HOOD: Made of flame-resistant Nomex, it covers the head, neck, chest, and shoulders.

PAD (Personal Alarm Device): This is a motion sensor with an alarm that starts chirping if the person wearing it doesn't move for thirty seconds. It alerts other firefighters to the possibilty of an unconscious crew member.

TURNOUT JACKET: This is made up of three layers: a flame-resistant Gortex shell, a vapor barrier, and an inner lining.

GLOVES: These are made of leather thick enough to hold a burning coal for up to five minutes without catching on fire.

TURNOUT PANTS: Turnout gear got its name because it's what firefighters wear when they "turn out" to fight a fire. The pants are made of the same layers as the jacket.

BOOTS: These may be waterproof leather or rubber. They have steel toes and bottoms to protect against sharp and heavy debris.

INTO THE FIRE

Tim didn't have on his SCBA (self-contained breathing apparatus), the portable air supply system he was supposed to wear when entering a smoke-filled building. The fire had already spread through most of the bedroom, so Tim didn't feel that there was time to go after this gear. He only took time to pull up his protective hood. Then he put his helmet on, hauled himself over the windowsill, and dropped to the floor.

As Tim crawled forward, he stayed low, with his face close to the carpet. Hot air rises, carrying smoke with it, so this was the coolest, least smoky air in the room. The smoke was making it hard to breathe, though. He also couldn't see much through the smoke, so he had to keep feeling around with one arm and then the other. He wished he had a Thermal Imaging System camera.

SEEING THROUGH SMOKE

Small enough to hold easily in one hand, the Thermal Imaging System camera (right) senses different degrees of temperature. Then, similar to a digital camera, it displays an image made up of areas of different temperatures on a screen. This reveals spots that are on fire, but it also can show a human or even an animal shape, based on body temperature. The camera is even able to sense areas of varying heat on the other side of solid objects, making it possible to look through walls. The Thermal Imaging System lets firefighters quickly check inside closets and cupboards—without opening doors—to find anyone who might be trying to hide to escape the fire.

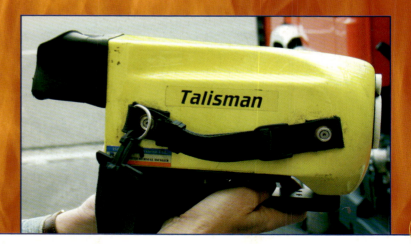

That would let him see Daishna through the smoke.

WHY IT'S BAD TO INHALE SMOKE

Being burned is the greatest danger in a fire. Next is breathing in smoke. Breathing smoke causes three different kinds of problems: heat damage, a decreased oxygen supply, and exposure to toxic chemicals. The full effects of the damage may take several days to show up. The first and most immediate danger is that smoky air contains less oxygen, the gas in the air that people need to live. Without enough oxygen, the body can't function properly and the person may die.

Because the smoky air is usually hot, it can burn and even destroy cells in the lining of the mouth and throat. About twenty-four hours after exposure to smoke, the damaged cells will give off fluids that can build up and again make it hard to breathe.

Smoke is also likely to contain chemicals given off by the different burning materials. These chemicals can trigger a chain reaction that may damage the person's immune system or kill cells in the lungs.

Statistics show that about 4 percent of fire victims die of their injuries. Many of those people die from smoke inhalation rather than from burns.

JUMPING TO SAFETY

Tim couldn't see the baby, but when she screamed again, he got a sense of where to search. Behind her cries, he could hear the crackling flames and the other firefighters at work. They were smashing windows and using a chain saw to cut a hole in the roof to let the smoke and heat escape.

Then suddenly Tim's fingers, reaching ahead of him in the smoke, went right into the little girl's mouth. He immediately pulled the child against his stomach, crawled back to the window, and jumped out. Behind him, the room exploded. The little girl was rushed to the UC Davis Medical Center, where she was treated for second- and third-degree burns and for smoke inhalation. Fortunately, she was well enough to be released two days later.

Tim Adams received a medal for saving baby Daishna's life.

AFTERWARD

Tim Adams continues to work as a firefighter for the Sacramento Fire Department. He has never seen Daishna again, but he's proud that he was there the day she needed him. Tim received the Gold Medal of Valor for saving Daishna's life. In earning this medal, he follows in the footsteps of his father. In 1963 Ernest Adams received the Gold Medal of Valor for rescuing three children from a burning apartment building.

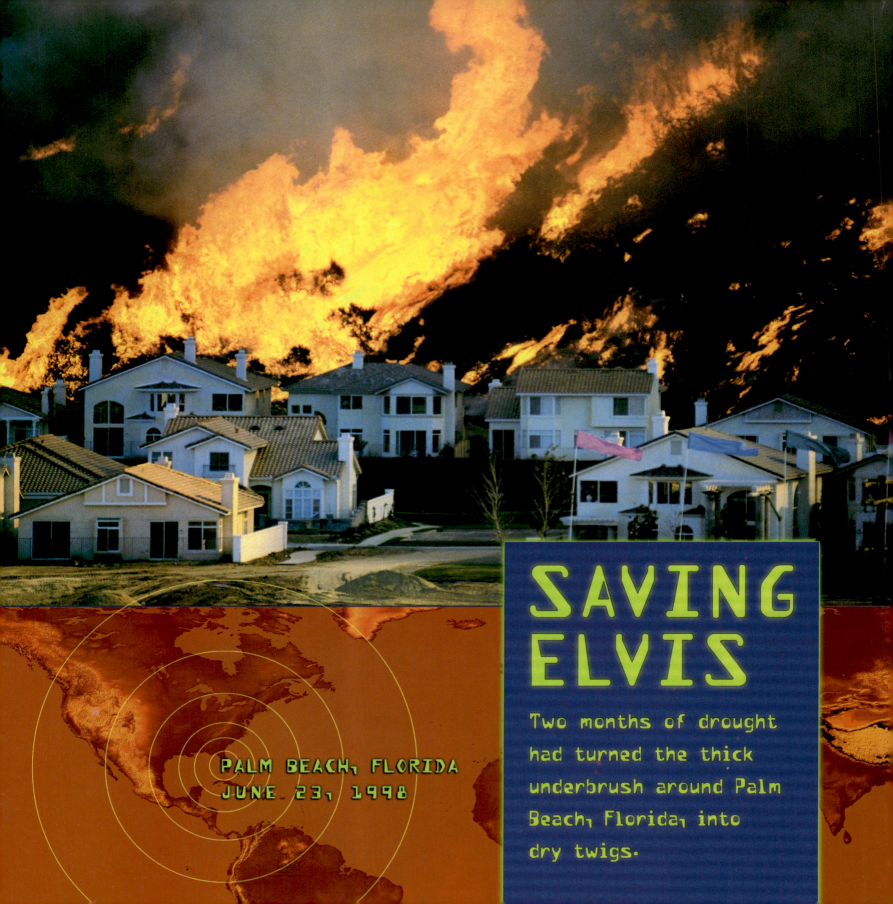

SAVING ELVIS

Two months of drought had turned the thick underbrush around Palm Beach, Florida, into dry twigs.

PALM BEACH, FLORIDA
JUNE 23, 1998

When a fire broke out in this brush, it quickly became a wall of flames. While some firefighting crews tried to put out the fire, others went from house to house, urging people to leave the danger zone.

Seeing the approaching flames, Jim and Debbie Hodges loaded a few belongings into their car and went to collect Elvis, their black Labrador

puppy. But as soon as he was unchained, Elvis fled into the hole he'd dug under his doghouse. Unable to budge the big doghouse from its sturdy foundation, Jim and Debbie were still trying to coax the puppy out when the firefighters arrived.

Luckily, John Bartlett was on this fire crew. Besides being a firefighter, he was also the inventor of Barricade Gel, a new spray-on, flame-resistant material.

Firefighters in Florida try to control a brush fire before it reaches homes.

DISPOSABLE DIAPERS

John got the idea for Barricade Gel when he discovered a dirty disposable diaper was the only thing completely undamaged in the remains of a house fire. The diaper was filled with liquid urine and was too wet to burn. Curious, he called a chemist to learn what chemical made the diaper able to

John Bartlett sprays Barricade Gel on a house to test its effectiveness.

trap liquid so effectively. He learned it was the same sort of highly absorbent chemical that is sometimes also added to flowerpots to soak up water and release it slowly. John and his father went to work in their garage. What they developed was a way to put the powdered chemical in an applicator attached to a hose. When water sprayed through the applicator, the chemical absorbed it. It became a gooey, water-saturated liquid that would coat whatever it touched. In tests, wood planks coated with the gooey liquid did not burn when thrown into a bonfire. It was as if soaking-wet sponges were stuck all over the pieces of wood.

Barricade Gel was still in the experimental stage when the fire crew arrived to evacuate Jim and Debbie Hodges. But John had convinced the fire department to give his new product a test. So the fire truck was equipped with the gel. When John learned about the Hodgeses' dog, he asked their permission to coat their house with the gooey liquid. Then he also sprayed Elvis's doghouse.

Elvis gets a pat from John (left), while Jim (right) looks on.

AFTERWARD

Almost twenty-four hours later, the fire died down enough for John to accompany Jim Hodges back to his home. Although other houses on the street were smoking ruins, the Hodgeses' house was just fine. So was the doghouse. To everyone's delight, Elvis rushed out to greet John and Jim.

In 2003, when brush fires raged in California, fire departments in San Diego County and Canyon County used Barricade Gel. Both departments reported that even when applied as much as eight hours before flames engulfed homes, the product still kept the buildings safe. When the fire danger was over, the gel was easily washed away with water. Barricade Gel has proved that a superabsorbent chemical can do more than just keep babies dry and houseplants watered.

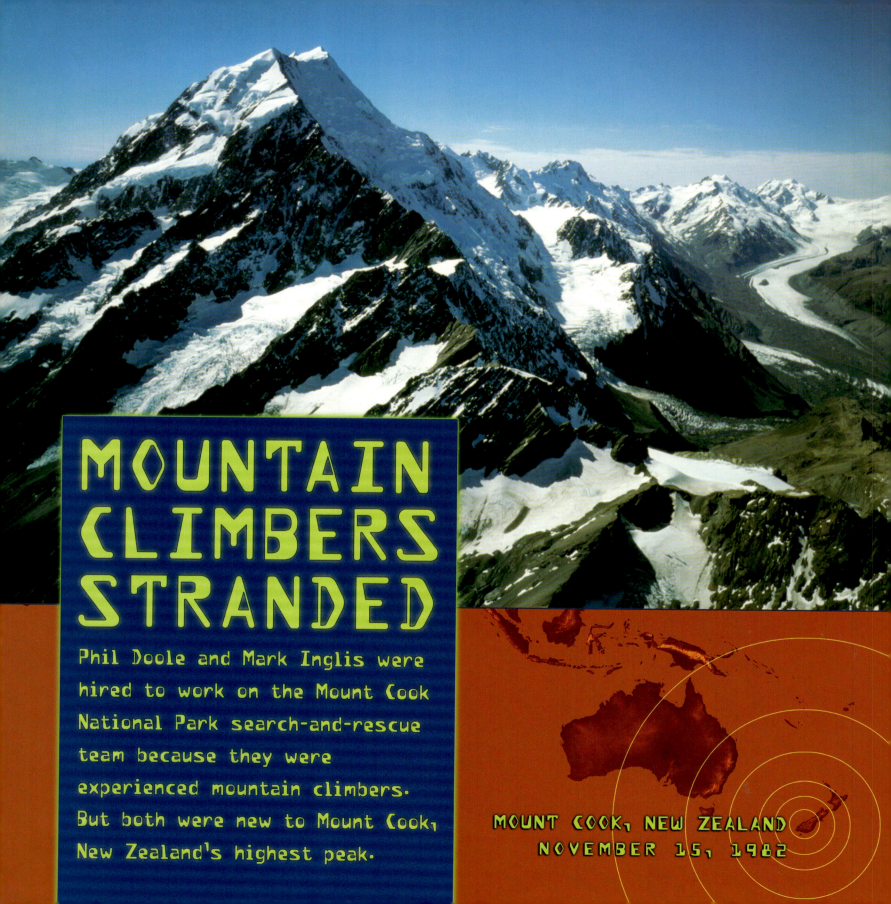

MOUNTAIN CLIMBERS STRANDED

Phil Doole and Mark Inglis were hired to work on the Mount Cook National Park search-and-rescue team because they were experienced mountain climbers. But both were new to Mount Cook, New Zealand's highest peak.

MOUNT COOK, NEW ZEALAND NOVEMBER 15, 1982

One day when the weather cleared after a storm, Mark suggested they climb to the summit. The pair made good time up the slope, but just before they could reach the snow-covered peak, the weather suddenly became stormy.

Because they had chosen to climb light—without heavy clothes, tents, much food, or even a radio—the two were in trouble. Spotting what looked like a cave, the pair climbed in to wait out the storm.

SEARCH IMPOSSIBLE

When the storm continued to rage after the first night, Phil and Mark needed water. The only way they could get a drink was to fill their water bottles with snow and tuck the bottles inside their clothes next to their warm skin to melt the snow. This used up precious body heat. They had trouble keeping warm because of the cold wind. What they had thought was a cave turned out to have an opening at the other end too. It was really a tunnel, and the wind roared through it.

When the two men didn't return from their climb, rescuers were alerted. Several days passed before the storm let up enough for a helicopter to reach a hut where rescuers thought the climbers had taken refuge. When they found the hut empty, most people assumed Mark and Phil must be dead. But the rescue team's leader, Bert Youngman, refused to give up. He ordered the team to climb the mountain in search of the pair. The rescue effort had to be delayed, however, because a fresh storm had rolled in.

DARING RESCUE

Phil and Mark were trapped near the top of the mountain for seven days before the skies finally cleared enough for the rescue team to launch a helicopter search. Even though they were too weak to climb down the mountain on their own, they managed to crawl out of the tunnel to wave at the circling helicopter. Spotting them, the rescuers dropped much-needed supplies: food, water, sleeping bags, and a portable stove.

Once again, a team prepared to climb up to rescue Mark and Phil, but another storm system moved in to stop them. Almost another week passed before the rescue effort could finally get under way.

By this time, the rescuers feared the climbers would need to be carried down on stretchers. A temporary camp was set up on a flat area about 3,000 feet (914 meters) below the summit. The plan was for a rescue team to carry the pair down from the tunnel to the temporary camp. A medical team waiting there would provide emergency treatment.

A rescue helicopter dropped food and other supplies to the stranded climbers.

STAYING ALIVE

The only food Phil Doole and Mark Inglis had with them was a couple of candy bars. That was all they had to eat during the first week they were trapped on the mountain.

The human body can continue to function for several weeks on its fat reserves, but a person will die in a few days without water. Water is in the body's juices that break down the stored fat so it can be used to nourish the body. Water is the main ingredient in the blood that carries the food nutrients throughout the body. Water also flushes wastes out of the body in urine and sweat. Phil and Mark had water bottles with them, and when the bottles were empty, they scooped up snow. Then they each tucked a bottle inside their clothes next to their skin. Imagine how cold it must have made them feel melting the snow with their body heat. Still this was the only way they could obtain the water they needed to stay alive.

After the helicopter dropped supplies, Phil and Mark had chocolate bars, fruit cookies, and some ready-to-eat ration packs to eat. But Phil said that after not having food for so long, it was hard to digest anything. They only ate a little at a time because eating made their stomachs ache. Even more than the food, they valued getting small tanks of gas and a gas-powered stove they could use to melt the snow.

A plane could land there to pick up the climbers and fly them to a hospital. While rescuers were being ferried to the temporary camp, one of the helicopters crashed. Luckily, none of the eight people on board was killed, but some were injured. For a while, the rescue effort had to shift to getting the injured rescue team to the hospital.

Finally, fearing yet another storm delay, Chief Youngman decided to try something daring. Even though there was no place to land, a helicopter could fly in close to the summit. A member of the rescue team would be carried to the mountaintop dangling on a rope from the helicopter. First, one of the climbers would be harnessed to the person on the rope and carried beneath the helicopter to the temporary camp. Then the helicopter and rescue team member would return for the other climber.

This type of helicopter rescue had

never before been attempted in New Zealand. Luckily, it was successful. Fourteen days after taking refuge in the ice tunnel, the climbers were finally able to leave the mountain.

Having artificial legs has not stopped Phil Doole from climbing mountains.

AFTERWARD

Unfortunately, because of severe frostbite, both Mark Inglis and Phil Doole lost their legs. Having artificial limbs hasn't slowed down either of them, though. Mark won a silver medal in the 1,000-meter cycling event at the Sydney 2000 Paralympics, a competition for the disabled. Phil Doole is still able to ski and climb mountains. In December 2003, Phil finally completed the climb he started in 1982. He returned to Mount Cook. This time, he made it all the way to the summit. And he climbed back down safely.

TSUNAMI STRIKES!

At around 11:00 A.M., Ned Kelly and his buddy Nick Ward had only just returned to their hotel from the beach on Phi Phi Island, Thailand.

PHI PHI ISLAND, THAILAND
DECEMBER 26, 2004

It was time to pick up their luggage and head to the dock. There, they planned to catch a boat taxi to the next island stop on their Christmas vacation. Suddenly, they heard shouting and rushed out onto the balcony. People were running away from the beach. Chasing after them was what looked like a trickle of water, oozing across the ground.

But within fifteen to twenty seconds, the water surged ashore, reaching a depth of 6 feet (about 2 meters). And there was no doubt about the force of the wave. Screams could be heard above the crashing, crunching, smashing sounds of the beachfront shops and wooden huts crumpling in its path. People were knocked over and pushed through shop windows. Debris was shoved over the top of people floundering in the water. Then everything—debris, dead bodies, and struggling survivors—was swept toward Ned and Nick's hotel, a two-story concrete block building.

Ned yanked off his belt, gave one end to Nick, and used the other to lower himself onto a rooftop. From there, he grabbed onto anyone in the wave who was within reach and handed the person up to Nick. He was able to pull eight people to safety.

Then as quickly as it had come in, the tsunami (a giant wave) receded, leaving people trapped under piles of wreckage. Ned and Nick rushed out to help the survivors.

They found Andy, who had been blasted out of a hut on the beach. He was covered with cuts and was bleeding badly. They found others to help them carry him back to the hotel. Alison had toe bones so badly broken they were poking out of her skin. One after another, they carried the survivors to the hotel, where they turned the rooms into a makeshift hospital.

In between trips, Ned sent a text message to his girlfriend: BIG TIDAL WAVE HIT THE ISLAND. LOADS DEAD. I'M OK SO FAR. To his surprise, she was able to call him on his cell phone. She said news reports warned another wave would strike the island in an hour.

Ned Kelly and Nick Ward used a blanket and metal poles as a stretcher to take injured people to their hotel-room hospital.

TSUNAMIS

Sometimes, forces within the earth cause one or more of the plates forming the earth's crust to shift, causing an earthquake. The plates under the Indian Ocean shifted on December 26, 2004. During this earthquake, one plate was suddenly thrust upward about 100 feet (30 meters). This upthrust created a series of powerful surface waves on the ocean above—the tsunami.

Like any ocean wave, the particles of water within each tsunami wave sweep around and around from the crest (top) to the trough (bottom). When the tsunami gets close to a coast, where the ocean is shallower, the circling water slows down as it drags across the bottom. When the front of the wave slows down, the water rushing behind it begins to pile up. The faster the wave is moving, the faster it piles up and the stronger its impact when it strikes land.

BEFORE

AFTER

Compare the before-and-after satellite images of Banda Aceh in Indonesia, and see the large areas that were damaged by the tsunami.

The December 26 tsunami that hit Ned and Nick was deadly. In all, waves struck eleven countries around the earthquake site. Indonesia, Thailand, Sri Lanka, India, and the Maldives were the closest to the earthquake. They were hit by the strongest waves and suffered the worst damage. Overall, the tsunami's death toll was more than 280,000 people, making it the deadliest tsunami in history. At least another 500,000 were injured, and thousands are missing.

STAYING ALIVE

Survivors who could walk streamed past the hotel, heading for Lookout Point, a low hill that was the highest point on Phi Phi. Ned and Nick could have joined them and escaped the beachfront, but they didn't. Ned said, "We looked around at the people we were with. There were just so many."

Nearly fifty injured people were in the hotel by that time. Ned said, "We couldn't carry them down the hotel stairs and up to Lookout Point. So it was a case of either you leave them and get there yourself or you stay with them and take your chances." The pair decided to keep everyone together and alive until help arrived. They moved all the wounded to the hotel's roof—the closest high ground.

THE LONG NIGHT

When an hour passed and another wave hadn't arrived, Ned and Nick went out searching for survivors again. After dark, they strapped on the lights that scuba divers wear for night dives and kept searching. Ned said, "The few times I actually lay down on the rooftop, I couldn't rest. I kept thinking, I've just got to have another look. Maybe I've missed somebody." The pair also collected bottles of water, canned food, bandages, and some medicines. Andy's many bleeding wounds were especially serious. They feared he was going to die before help could reach Phi Phi Island.

During the night, some of the survivors returned to the beach. When a couple of local boats arrived,

Ned (above) waits for Nick to help carry a stretcher full of water, food, and other supplies. To escape Phi Phi Island, people crowded aboard a small motorboat.

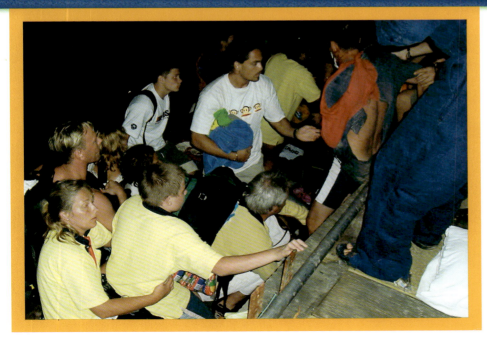

people crowded onto the dock, which, amazingly, was still standing. People fought to get onto the slim wooden motorboats, which normally held only five or six passengers. Then the overloaded boats chugged slowly into the night.

71

THE EVACUATION

In the morning, helicopters arrived to carry away the most seriously wounded, and Andy was rescued. Then several big boats arrived. Ned and Nick took one of these boats to Krabi, on the mainland, just an hour's ride away. They were surprised to discover the tsunami had caused no damage at all there. Ned said, "It was frustrating to see it go in just one hour from civilization to a nightmare." From Krabi, the two friends took the first available flight to Bangkok, Thailand, and then flew home to London, England.

Helicopters arrived to carry the wounded to hospitals.

Tsunami Early Warning System

An early warning system in parts of the Pacific Ocean can detect tsunamis and issue warnings, but its scope is limited. The goal is to expand this Pacific Ocean system and establish systems in both the Atlantic and Indian oceans.

The early warning system begins with sensors in the ocean. Each sensor is made up of a surface buoy and a pressure sensor anchored to the seafloor. The pressure sensor is so sensitive it can detect a change in the water depth as small as a fraction of an inch (a few millimeters). The pressure sensor transmits this depth information by sound signals to the surface buoy. The surface buoy sends the data to satellites circling the earth. Scientists in early warning centers analyze this information from the satellites. When the early warning center receives information that shows a tsunami forming, computers produce a model of the tsunami's expected path. Then a warning is issued to all the island nations and countries with coastal cities where the tsunami might strike.

A surface buoy (above) and its underwater pressure sensor (right) are the sensing devices for a tsunami early warning system.

AFTERWARD

Life is little different than it was before the tsunami for Ned Kelly and Nick Ward. Ned is on the job again, working as a police officer dealing with traffic accidents. Nick runs his own engraving business. They continue to hear from many of the people they rescued, and they're still dealing with the memories of what happened. Ned said, "In my service as a police officer, I've dealt with death and trauma many times. But to find yourself in the thick of it when it's happened at such an incredible scale is something else. I can't put my hand over my heart and say I am over it. It's going to take a long, long time before things settle down."

In the countries where coastal villages and towns were destroyed by the tsunami, aid has switched from rescue to recovery. Governments and private aid groups are supplying funds and experts to build housing, provide new fishing boats, and restore services so that people who stayed and those who fled inland can begin to live normal lives.

SURVIVING KATRINA

At 6:10 A.M local time on Monday, August 29, 2005, Hurricane Katrina slammed ashore near Buras, Louisiana, just 30 miles (48 kilometers) south of New Orleans, along the Gulf of Mexico.

NEW ORLEANS, LOUISIANA
AUGUST 29, 2005

All along the Gulf Coast, ships and floating oil rigs (platforms for drilling oil undersea) were shoved ashore. Many buildings were blown apart by the force of the storm.

With 145-mile-per-hour (233-kilometer-per-hour) winds and sheets of rain, Katrina roared into New Orleans. The winds overturned dumpsters and pushed cars along streets. Chunks of roofs, loose boards, road signs, and other debris were hurled into buildings. Giant trees fell, crashing through roofs and smashing cars. Power lines snapped and transmission towers toppled, cutting off electricity throughout much of the city.

At the city's Tulane University Hospital, the lights blinked, signaling the backup generators had just switched on. Karen Nelson, a nurse in the Pediatric Intensive Care Unit, hurried to check on fifteen-year old William. William's heart was giving out, and he needed a new one. Until a new heart was found, his life depended on the 500-pound (226-kilogram) artificial heart-assist machine attached to his chest. Karen was relieved to see the machine hadn't missed a beat when the generator switched on. Then she heard reports that the storm had passed through the city. The hospital apparently had withstood nature's worse punch with little more than a few broken windows and some roof damage. But that was about to change.

New Orleans is built on land that is lower than the sea and lake water around it. A series of walls made of earth or concrete, called levees, holds back the water. Some of the concrete levees protect New Orleans from Lake Pontchartrain, just north of the city. Katrina's storm surge—a wall of water plowed ashore by the strong winds—broke openings in the Lake Pontchartrain levees. Water began to pour into the city. Tulane University Hospital quickly became an island

surrounded by water. Then water started pouring into the first floor of the hospital.

EVACUATE!

By Tuesday morning, people who had survived the storm were fleeing the flooding city. Some trapped by rapidly rising water were forced to take refuge on cars and rooftops. The Tulane Hospital management decided that patients, visiting parents, and staff—more than one thousand people altogether—would have to be evacuated. Government agencies did not respond to calls for help. So the hospital managers hired private helicopters to rescue the most critically

People waded through rising floodwaters on Canal Street (above) in New Orleans. A rescue team helps a family (below) that took refuge on the roof of their SUV after they were caught on a flooded highway.

ill patients. The hospital staff began to prepare the patients.

Karen said, "It was absolutely chaos. Seeing all of this, William was afraid. He knew that if anything happened to his machine he would die. I told him I'd tell him when to worry, but that for now he was safe."

Hurricanes

Hurricanes are the earth's biggest storm systems. They form over warm tropical oceans when the surface water warms up enough for a lot of water to evaporate. And the warm, moist air quickly rises high enough to cool, forming thunderstorm clouds—a whole cluster of them that merges into one storm system. When the winds in this system blow steadily at 75 miles (119 kilometers) per hour, this storm is classified as a hurricane. The force of the earth's spinning, called the Coriolis force, makes the hurricane winds turn. In the center, warm, dry air surges downward and pushes outward, creating the eye, a center area of calm surrounded by a wall of clouds. The storm's winds are strongest around the center.

Some hurricanes are stronger than others. Scientists have created a scale to rate a hurricane's strength from 1 (weakest) to 5 (strongest). Hurricane Katrina was ranked as a Category 4 when it struck Louisiana and the nearby Gulf Coast.

Scientists working on a research project called CAMEX (Convection and Moisture Experiment) want to learn more about conditions inside a hurricane. They are using satellites and high-flying planes loaded with special instruments to collect data from high up in the hurricane. They're also using robotic aircraft, called aerosondes, to fly through the lower, fiercest part of the storm and measure conditions there. With better understanding of hurricanes, researchers hope to be able to predict more precisely how intense the storm will be when it strikes land. Then emergency crews can be better prepared to help communities in the path of especially powerful storms.

eye

This photograph of a hurricane shows the eye, the calm center of the storm.

Tulane Hospital had never before needed to land a helicopter on the roof and didn't have a helipad. The hospital directors decided the roof of the parking garage connected to the hospital would work as a landing site. Teams of workers carried the young patients from the fourth-floor pediatric unit to the second-floor sky bridge. The team then took the children across the bridge to the hospital's parking garage and up to the roof. The helicopter rescues went smoothly until, suddenly, shots rang out. Snipers hiding in other buildings were shooting at the helicopters and the people. The evacuation had to be halted until the shooting stopped.

That night the generators ran out of fuel, so the hospital was without power. Fortunately, the hospital had a small generator, and it was plugged in to keep William's artificial heart-assist device working.

Helicopters evacuated patients and staff from the roof of the parking garage at Tulane University Hospital.

TEAM EFFORT

On Wednesday William's rescue became everyone's focus. A battery pack with a one-hour charge was hooked up to keep the heart-assist machine operating during the trip to the garage roof. Since the elevators were no longer working, a team of men carried William, the heavy heart-assist machine, and the battery pack all the way to the garage roof. Karen went along in case the battery pack failed. If that happened, she would have to use hand pumps to take over the machine's job until power could be restored. But everything went well. Once the helicopter's door closed, its power supply took over operating the heart-assist machine, and William was on his way to safety.

SUPERDOME

Before Hurricane Katrina struck, about twenty thousand people sought safety in the Superdome, New Orleans's huge, covered sports stadium. Many of these people were too poor to have cars to drive out of the city or were too frail to leave. What seemed like a good shelter soon became a terrible place to be. The storm's powerful winds

ripped two holes in the Superdome's roof, showering the people inside with debris and rain. More water leaked into elevator shafts and stairwells, making floors wet and slippery. Then the power failed. The toilets stopped working. Trash piled up everywhere. The Superdome became a super hot, stinky horror. People vomited, fainted, had heart attacks, and suffered other medical problems. Some pregnant women gave birth. Five days later, buses finally arrived to take away the thousands of stranded people. But they had to wait in huge lines to leave the ruined Superdome.

On Thursday, helicopters continued to carry away the critical care patients. Boats also arrived and ferried less critical patients, parents, and some hospital staff to safety.

By dark, Karen was one of the few remaining staff members still to be rescued. She and the others went to the parking garage to be ready for the helicopter they were told was coming in the morning.

Some patients and hospital staff moved out by boat (above). Fiery explosions at refineries and warehouses (below) lit up the New Orleans's sky.

BOOM!

It was nearly 4:00 A.M. when an explosion shook the parking garage. Karen and the others jumped up and stared in disbelief. An orange fireball was lighting up the sky. Although they did not know what was burning at the time, a warehouse had exploded. They watched the flames and wondered if the whole city might catch fire and if they would ever be rescued.

Daylight came, and hours dragged by with no helicopter. Finally, an army Chinook helicopter arrived, and Karen and the others climbed aboard. It had been five long, difficult days since Hurricane Katrina had struck. Karen had helped see that her patients, including William, were rescued. Now, she too was safe.

AFTERWARD

William was moved to another pediatric intensive care hospital well outside the hurricane-damaged area. Karen lost her car and her home to Hurricane Katrina. She's currently staying with her family in Portland, Oregon, and looking for a job there. Karen has not decided if she will return to New Orleans once the city is cleaned up and rebuilt. She said, "It wasn't until later when I saw the city [New Orleans] on TV that I realized how fortunate we were to get out and that our [hospital] had really gone way above and beyond to get us out. Through it all, the nurses on my team stuck together, determined to go out together—and we did."

AS ALL OF THEIR STORIES SHOW, IN THE FACE OF LIFE-THREATENING DANGER, PEOPLE FIND THE COURAGE TO FACE AMAZING CHALLENGES. They use their understanding of how the world works, their ability to consider possible solutions, and their natural creativity to survive on their own or until help arrives. Sometimes, the saving edge comes from tools, like the GPS unit, or special materials, like Barricade Gel. But above all, it's people's indomitable spirit that helps those at risk stay alive. This spirit gives hardworking heroes a chance to accomplish amazing rescues.

GLOSSARY

avalanche: a large mass of snow sliding swiftly down a mountainside

barricade: something that blocks or stops something else from passing beyond a certain point

cells: the building blocks that make up all living things

CPR (cardiopulmonary resuscitation): a method of pushing on a victim's chest and breathing into the mouth, in rhythm, to keep blood moving and carry oxygen through the body until the heart can do it again without help

debris: the broken remains of an object or objects

drought: a prolonged period of dry weather that can damage or kill plants

evacuation: the rescue and removal of people in danger

frostbite: damage caused by exposure of living tissue to extreme cold

GPS (Global Positioning System) unit: a small computer that connects to satellites circling the earth to pinpoint the position of the person holding it

hypothermia: the condition of being below normal body temperature

keel: a part of a boat that extends underwater to keep it from rolling over

levee: a wall made to hold back water

mine shaft: a tunnel dug by miners through the earth in order to make it possible to remove minerals, coal, or other natural resources

organ: a part of the human body that has a special job to do, such as the heart, the lungs, or the stomach

Richter scale: a scale from 1 to 10 for measuring the amount of energy released by an earthquake. The higher the number, the stronger the quake. Each numerical increase represents a quake thirty-two times stronger than the previous one.

rubble: a mixture of broken concrete, wood, glass, and other debris

rudder: a device that steers a ship

scent receptor: the part of the nose that picks up smells and sends messages about them to the brain

transceiver: a device a person can wear to send signals to rescuers if he or she is caught in an avalanche

SOURCE NOTES

8   Patti Burnett, telephone interview with author, September 1, 2003.

14   Dr. Allan De Caen, telephone interview with author, September 7, 2003.

22   Sean Isgan, telephone interview with author, September 7, 2003.

21, 26, 28, 29   Randy Fogle, telephone interview with author, September 11, 2003.

37, 38   Tony Bullimore, telephone interview with author, September 17, 2003.

42, 43, 45   Robert Dube, telephone interview with author, May 18, 2005.

50, 51   Tim Adams, telephone interview with author, August 29, 2003.

70, 72, 74   Andrew (Ned) Kelly, telephone interview with author, April 28, 2005.

77, 82   Karen Nelson, telephone interview with author, September 12, 2005.

MORE INFORMATION

BOOKS

Gorrell, Gena Kinton. *Catching Fire: The Story Of Firefighting.* Toronto: Tundra Books, 1999. A history from bucket brigades to state-of-the-art, modern firefighting.

Kramer, Stephen. *Avalanche.* Minneapolis: Carolrhoda Books, Inc., 1992. Here is information about avalanches and their causes.

Lyons, Lewis. *Rescues at Sea with the U.S. and Canadian Coast Guards.* Brookshire, TX: Mason Crest Publishers, 2003. These real-life stories tell of rescues at sea.

Markle, Sandra. *Can You Believe: Amazing Earth: Earthquakes.* New York: Scholastic, 2002. Learn all there is to know about amazing earthquakes.

———. *Can You Believe? Hurricanes.* New York: Scholastic, 2002. Explore why hurricanes form, how they are tracked, and ways scientists are working to help people stay safe.

Morris, Ann, and Heidi J. Larson. *Tsunami: Helping Each Other.* Minneapolis: Millbrook Press, 2005. A firsthand account of two boys who survived the 2004 tsunami.

Presnall, Judith Janda. *Rescue Dogs.* Farmington Hills, MI: Thomson Gale, 2003. Investigate rescue dogs in action in disaster situations.

Souza, D. M. *Hurricanes.* Minneapolis: Carolrhoda Books, Inc., 1996. This explains how hurricanes form and the damage they do.

———. *Powerful Waves.* Minneapolis: Carolrhoda Books, Inc., 1992. This book discusses the formation, power, and destructive possibilities of tsunamis.

WEBSITES

Beartooth Search Dogs

http://www.montanasearchdogs.com/articles/ravalli_dog_course.htm
Discover dogs in training to rescue avalanche victims.

FEMA for Kids: Hurricanes

http://www.fema.gov/kids/hurr.htm
This website contains information, quizzes, and games to help children understand hurricanes.

Miami Museum of Science:
Hurricane Storm Science

http://www.miamisci.org/hurricane/
Here are activities demonstrating how hurricane storm systems work and how scientists study them. It also includes survivors' stories.

SELECTED BIBLIOGRAPHY

TELEPHONE INTERVIEWS WITH AUTHOR

Adams, Tim, August 29, 2003.

Bullimore, Tony, September 17, 2003.

Burnett, Patti, September 1, 2003.

De Caen, Allan, September 7, 2003.

Dube, Robert, May 18, 2005.

Fogle, Randy, September 11, 2003.

Hood, Robbie, September 19, 2005

Isgan, Sean, September 7, 2003.

Kelly, Andrew (Ned), April 28, 2005.

Nelson, Karen, September 12, 2005.

BOOKS

Bullimore, Tony. *Saved.* Boston: Little, Brown, 1997.

Burnett, Patti. *Avalanche/Hasty Search: The Care and Training of Avalanche Search and Rescue Dogs.* Irvine, CA: Doral Publishing, 2003.

Fredericks, Anthony D. *Tsunami Man: Learning about Killer Waves with Walter Dudley.* Honolulu: University of Hawaii Press, 2002.

NEWSPAPERS

Pittsburgh Post-Gazette. "The Quecreek Mine Rescue." *post-gazette.com.* August 6, 2002. http://www.post-gazette.com/localnews/20020729mineindex9.asp (August 31, 2005).

Reno Gazette Journal. "Dirty Diaper Sparked Idea for Fire-Blocking Gel." *RGJ.com.* July 25, 2002. http://www.rgj.com/news/stories/html/2002/07/25/20103.php (August 31, 2005).

Sacramento Bee. "Firefighter Pulls Child From Blazing Home." B1. *Sacbee.com.* December 23, 1994. http://nl.newsbank.com/ (August 31, 2005).

WEBSITES

ABC News Technology & Science

Dye, Lee. "New Technology Could Help Search Wreckage: High Tech Devices to Search Wreckage Could Help Even More in the Future." *ABC News.* August 1, 2005. http://abcnews.go.com/Technology/story?id=98259&page=1 (August 31, 2005).

Barricade Fire Blocking Gel

"Barricade Gel: Fire Protection through Technology." *Barricade Gel.* n.d. http://www.barricadegel.com/ (August 31, 2005).

BBC.CO.UK

"1997: Bullimore Rescued after 5 Days." *BBC.CO.UK.* January 9, 1997. http://news.bbc.co.uk/onthisday/hi/dates/stories/january/9/newsid_2518000/2518229.stm (August 31, 2005).

CBC News

"Edmonton Toddler Needs Surgery on Frostbitten Feet." *CBC News.* March 11, 2001. http://cbc.ca/cgibin/templates/view.cgi?category=Canada&%20story=/news/2001/03/11/erika_update010311 (August 31, 2005).

CBS News

"Miners Stuck Together." *CBS News.* July 29, 2002. http://www.cbsnews.com/stories/2002/07/29/national/main516690.shtml (August 31, 2005).

CNN.com

"Quecreek Miner Miracle: Teamwork Helped Miners Survive Underground" *CNN.com.* July 28, 2002. http://premium.europe.cnn.com/2002/US/07/28/mine.accident/ (August 31, 2005).

Coal Age

Fiscor, Steve. "Quecreek Rescuers Save Nine Trapped Miners." *Coal Age.* September 1, 2002. http://coalage.com/ar/coal_quecreek_rescuers_save/index.htm (August 31, 2005).

CTV News with Lloyd Robertson

"Cold That Nearly Killed Toddlers Also Helped Save Their Lives." *CTV.ca.* April 17, 2001. http://www.ctv.ca/servlet/ArticleNews/story/CTVNews/1027384006139_22793206/ (August 31, 2005).

First Special Response Group

First Special Response Group. 2002. http://www.1srg.org/ (September 6, 2005).

National Geographic News

Trivedi, Bijal P. "Search-and-Rescue Robots Tested at New York Disaster Site." *National Geographic News.* September 14, 2001. http://news.nationalgeographic.com/news/2001/09/0914_TVdisasterrobot.html (August 31, 2005).

NOAA Tsunami Research Program

"PMEL Tsunami Research Program." *NOAA.* May 13, 2005. http://www.pmel.noaa.gov/tsunami (September 6, 2005).

Solar Navigator

"Tony Bullimore—Oryx Quest." *Solar Navigator.* December 9, 2004. http://www.solarnavigator.net/tony_bullimore.htm (August 31, 2005).

Sri Chinmoy Marathon Team U.S.A.

"Amputee Climber Phil Doole Reaches Summit." *Sri Chinmoy Marathon Team U.S.A.* April 24, 2004. http://www.srichinmoyraces.org/us/transcendence/climbing_feats/paststoriesclimbing/amputee_climber_phil_doole_reaches_summit (August 31, 2005).

INDEX

PHOTO ACKNOWLEDGMENTS

FROM THE AUTHOR

Rescues! was inspired by my own personal experience. In 1998 I was camping with two scientists at a remote research site in Antarctica in order to observe and photograph Adélie penguins raising their young. Unexpectedly, a fierce storm struck with hurricane-force winds, freezing temperatures, and blowing snow. Our tents were shredded. We had to take shelter in our sleeping bags to wait for a break in the storm that would allow a helicopter to reach us. Surviving the storm and knowing the joy of being rescued was an experience I'll never forget. Because of this, I was deeply moved by the stories of the rescuers and the survivors whose personal experiences are told in this book. Take another look at the photos in *Rescues!* to see what hardships people endured, what efforts people went to, and what a joyous moment each rescue was for everyone involved.

Sandra Markle is a former elementary school science teacher, a nationally known science education consultant, and the author of many award-winning books for children. Her series include Animal Predators—a *Booklist* top ten series—and Animal Scavengers.